HUMPBACK WHALE
MARVELOUS MUSICIAN

PAIGE V. POLINSKY

CONSULTING EDITOR, DIANE CRAIG, M.A./READING SPECIALIST

Super Sandcastle

An Imprint of Abdo Publishing
abdopublishing.com

abdopublishing.com

Published by Abdo Publishing, a division of ABDO, PO Box 398166, Minneapolis, Minnesota 55439. Copyright © 2017 by Abdo Consulting Group, Inc. International copyrights reserved in all countries. No part of this book may be reproduced in any form without written permission from the publisher. Super SandCastle™ is a trademark and logo of Abdo Publishing.

Printed in the United States of America, North Mankato, Minnesota
062016
092016

Editor: Rebecca Felix
Content Developer: Nancy Tuminelly
Cover and Interior Design and Production: Christa Schneider, Mighty Media, Inc.
Photo Credits: iStockphoto; Mighty Media, Inc.; Shutterstock

Library of Congress Cataloging-in-Publication Data

Names: Polinsky, Paige V., author.
Title: Humpback whale : marvelous musician / by Paige V. Polinsky.
Description: Minneapolis, Minnesota : Abdo Publishing, [2017] | Series:
  Animal superstars
Identifiers: LCCN 2016006320 (print) | LCCN 2016007328 (ebook) | ISBN
  9781680781496 (print) | ISBN 9781680775921 (ebook)
Subjects: LCSH: Humpback whale--Juvenile literature.
Classification: LCC QL737.C424 P65 2016 (print) | LCC QL737.C424 (ebook) |
  DDC 599.5/25--dc23
LC record available at http://lccn.loc.gov/2016006320

Super SandCastle™ books are created by a team of professional educators, reading specialists, and content developers around five essential components—phonemic awareness, phonics, vocabulary, text comprehension, and fluency—to assist young readers as they develop reading skills and strategies and increase their general knowledge. All books are written, reviewed, and leveled for guided reading, early reading intervention, and Accelerated Reader™ programs for use in shared, guided, and independent reading and writing activities to support a balanced approach to literacy instruction.

CONTENTS

SEA GIANTS

Humpback whales are **mammals**. They are huge. Adult humpbacks weigh about 80,000 pounds (36,000 kg). They can grow to 63 feet (19 m) long.

48 to 63 FEET
(15 to 19 M)

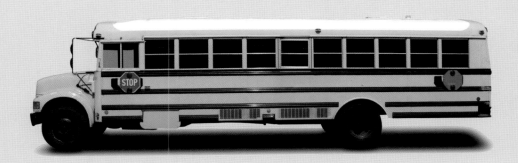

HUMPBACK WHALES CAN GROW LONGER THAN A SCHOOL BUS!

FINS AND TAILS

Humpbacks have long flippers. Their **dorsal** fins are small. Humpback tail fins are called flukes. Each whale's flukes look different.

FLIPPERS

DORSAL FIN

FLUKES

SUPER SINGERS

Male humpbacks create songs. They use **moans** and squeaks. Some songs are short. Others can last 35 minutes. Humpbacks can sing for more than 24 hours straight!

WHALE SONGS

HUMPBACK SONGS GROW AND CHANGE OVER TIME.

MYSTERY MUSIC

Nobody knows why humpbacks sing. It may be to communicate. Sometimes humpbacks sing together. And neighboring humpbacks sing similar songs.

COAST **TO COAST**

Humbacks live in every ocean. In summer, they feed in polar waters. They travel to warmer waters in winter. This trip is thousands of miles!

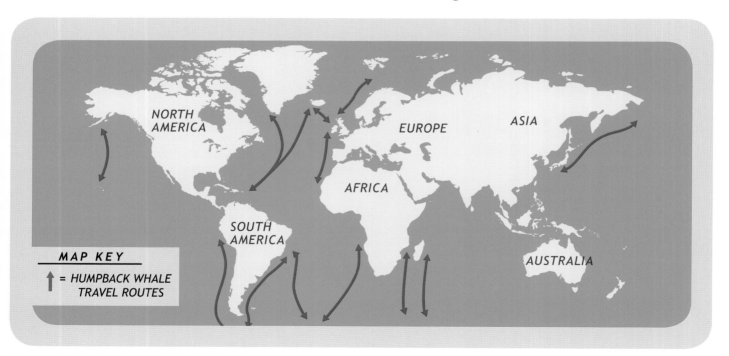

NORTH
AMERICA

EUROPE

ASIA

AFRICA

SOUTH
AMERICA

AUSTRALIA

MAP KEY

↑ = HUMPBACK WHALE
TRAVEL ROUTES

HUNGRY HUMPBACKS

Humpbacks eat **krill** and **plankton**. They catch food with their **baleen**. A humpback eats up to 3,000 pounds (1,400 kg) of food per day.

*BALEEN IS **TOUGH** AND SPRINGY.*

FISH FRENZY

HUMPBACKS TRAP AND EAT FISH. BIRDS OFTEN JOIN THE FEAST!

JUMPING GIANTS

Humpbacks leap into the air. They use their strong tails to push up out of the water. This is called breaching. It causes quite a splash!

HUMPBACKS SOMETIMES TWIRL WHILE BREACHING.

BIG BABIES

A female humpback births one baby about every three years. Females nurse their calves for nearly one year. Adult humpbacks often travel alone. Some travel in small groups.

HOW BIG?

BABY HUMPBACKS ARE UP TO 15 FEET (5 M) LONG AT BIRTH!

HUMAN DANGER

Many people used to hunt humpbacks. They sold their meat. Humpbacks nearly went **extinct**. Today, people are not allowed to sell humpback meat. Humpback populations are growing.

PEOPLE HAVE MADE OIL FROM HUMPBACK WHALE FAT.

HUMPBACK WHALE SUPERSTAR

Can you imagine a humpback whale superstar? What **awards** would it win?

WHAT DO YOU KNOW ABOUT
HUMPBACK WHALES?

1. All humpback flukes look the same.

True or false?

2. Humpbacks can sing for more than 24 hours.

True or false?

3. Humpbacks travel to cold waters for the winter.

True or false?

4. Breaching is when a humpback leaps out of the water.

True or false?

ANSWERS:
1. FALSE 2. TRUE 3. FALSE 4. TRUE

GLOSSARY

AWARD - a prize.

BALEEN - a material hanging from the upper jaws of some kinds of whales. Whales use baleen to catch food.

DORSAL - positioned near or on the back of an animal.

EXTINCT - no longer existing.

KRILL - very small creatures that live in the ocean.

MAMMAL - a warm-blooded animal that has hair and whose females produce milk to feed their young.

MOAN - a long, low sound.

PLANKTON - very tiny animal and plant organisms that live in water.

TOUGH - strong but flexible.